Witch, Goblin, and Ghost's BOOK OF THINGS TO DO

Five I AM READING *Stories*

by Sue Alexander
pictures by Jeanette Winter

PANTHEON BOOKS

This book is dedicated with
milk, cookies, and love to
Gray Johnson Poole

MANY THANKS TO SID FLEISCHMAN
WHO DESIGNED THE MAGIC TRICK
ESPECIALLY FOR GOBLIN

Library of Congress Cataloging in Publication Data
Alexander, Sue, 1933- Witch, Goblin, and Ghost's book of things to do.
(An I am reading book) Summary: Three friends show how to
write a rebus, play a game, write in secret code, put on a play,
and perform a magic trick.
1. Games—Juvenile literature.   2. Amusements— Juvenile literature. [1. Amusements]
I. Winter, Jeanette.   II. Title.
GV1203.A39   1983   793   80-28930
ISBN 0-394-84612-5   ISBN 0-394-94612-X (lib. bdg.)

THE STORIES

GHOST'S REBUS

Ghost was sitting near his tree.

Goblin came along.

"Hello, Ghost," he said.

"What are you doing?"

"I'm writing a story," Ghost said.

And he showed it to Goblin.

"What kind of story is this?"

asked Goblin.

"There are pictures

where some of the words should be!"

"It's called a rebus," Ghost said.

"See if you can read it, Goblin."

This is the story Goblin read:

Once there was a

who was flying a .

Suddenly the broke.

And the sailed away in the wind.

The ran after the .

And he bumped into a .

"Hello ," said the .

"Have U seen my ?"

5

"No!" roared the .

And the climbed a

to look for .

The went on.

He saw an .

"Hello ," said the .

"Have you seen my ?"

"No!" hooted the .

And the flew

2 the of the .

"Oh ," said the

" 'll never find my .

Just then a came along.

She was on her .

" know where your is,"

said the .

"Get on my ✦

and 👁 will take U there."

The 😊 got on the 🧙's ✦.

The 🧙 flew her ✦

over the 🌳🌳🌳.

She flew her ✦

past a flock of 🐦🐦🐦.

She flew her ✦

into a ☁ .

"There is your 🪁!" she said.

Then the 🧙 took the 😊

and his 🪁

back 2 the meadow.

And the 😊 and the 🧙

took turns flying the 🪁.

The end.

"Ghost," said Goblin,

"that rebus story was fun to read."

"It was fun to write, too,"

said Ghost.

"Do you think I could write one?"

Goblin asked.

"Of course you can, Goblin,"

said Ghost.

"Anyone can."

GOBLIN'S MYSTERY BAG

Witch and Goblin were in Goblin's cave.

"Witch, I know a game we can play,"
Goblin said.

"Oh, good!" said Witch.

"You stay here," Goblin said,

"and I will go and get

what we need to play the game."

Goblin got a paper bag

and put ten things in it.

He got a big handkerchief.

Then he came back

and put the bag on the table.

"What is the bag for, Goblin?"

asked Witch.

"This is a mystery bag," Goblin said.

"I'm going to blindfold you, Witch.

Then you put your hand in the bag.

You feel the things inside

and tell me what they are."

"All right," said Witch.

Goblin tied the handkerchief

over Witch's eyes.

"Can you see me, Witch?" Goblin asked.

"No," said Witch.

"I can't see anything!"

"Good!" said Goblin.

"Here's the bag, Witch."

And he put her hand inside the bag.

"Oh!" Witch yelled.

She pulled her hand out of the bag.

"There's a worm in there, Goblin!"

"No there isn't," Goblin said.

And he laughed.

Witch put her hand back into the bag.

She felt all the things inside.

Then she took her hand out.

Goblin untied the blindfold.

"Now tell me what's inside the bag,"
he said.

"Are you *sure* there isn't
a worm in there?" Witch asked.

"I'm sure," Goblin said.

"Well, it felt like a worm,"
Witch said.

Goblin laughed again.

"What else did you feel
inside the bag?" he asked.

Witch thought for a minute.

"A thimble and a spoon," she said.

Goblin took a thimble out of the bag.

He took out a spoon.

And he put them on the table.

"A pencil is in there, too,"

Witch said.

"And a tiny bottle."

Goblin took a pencil and a bottle

out of the bag.

"So far, so good, Witch," he said.

"What else is inside?"

"Hmmm," said Witch.

And she thought some more.

"I think there's a ring in the bag,"

Witch said, "and a little book, too."

Goblin took a ring and a little book

out of the bag.

He put them on the table.

Witch walked back and forth

while she thought some more.

Then she stopped.

"Oh!" she said.

"I felt a bell in there, too!"

"You're right, Witch," Goblin said.

And he took the bell out of the bag.

Witch thought and thought.

Then she said, "Goblin are you *sure*

there isn't a worm in there?

Maybe it got in

when you weren't looking."

Goblin laughed.

Then he reached in the bag

and pulled out

a piece of cold, cooked spaghetti.

"Here's your worm, Witch," he said.

Witch laughed.

"You fooled me, Goblin," she said.

Then Goblin took two more things

out of the bag.

One was a piece of chalk.

The other was a seashell.

"That's a good game," Witch said.

"Let's play it again, Goblin.

And this time *I'll* fill

the mystery bag!"

A PLAY

"Let's put on a play today,"

Ghost said.

"That's a good idea, Ghost,"

said Witch.

"Which play should we put on?"

asked Goblin.

"Let's make one up," said Ghost.

"Any story can be made into a play.

Think about the stories you know."

Goblin thought.

So did Witch.

Then Goblin said, "Let's make a play

out of *Rumplestiltskin*.

It's one of my favorite stories."

"Yes, let's!" said Witch.

"I like that story, too!"

"All right," said Ghost.

"Witch, you can be the girl

who becomes the queen.

Goblin, you can be Rumplestiltskin.

And I'll be the narrator

who tells the story."

"Oh good!" Goblin said.

Witch, Goblin, and Ghost

read the Rumplestiltskin story.

They decided

what each of them would say.

Then Witch got a bracelet and a doll.

Ghost got a table

and a chair.

Goblin got some paper

and cut it into strips.

"This will be the straw," he said.

"What will we use for gold?"

asked Witch.

"How about a box

with the word GOLD on it?" said Ghost.

"That will work very well!"

Goblin said.

And he got a box.

Witch wrote the word GOLD on it.

"I think we have everything now,"

said Ghost.

"Then let's begin!"

said Goblin and Witch together.

And this is the play

Witch, Goblin, and Ghost put on:

Narrator:

Once there was a girl

whose father told the king

that she could spin straw into gold.

The king liked gold.

So he took the girl to his castle.

He gave her some straw

and sent her to the spinning room.

Girl:

(She comes in carrying the straw.

She puts it on the table.)

Oh dear! What am I to do?

I don't know how

to spin straw into gold!

(She sits down on the chair

and begins to cry.)

Rumplestiltskin: (He comes in.)

Don't cry. I can help you.

Girl: (She jumps up in surprise.)

Oh! Who are you?

Rumplestiltskin:

I won't tell you.

But if you give me a present,

I will turn the straw into gold.

Girl:

All I have is my bracelet.

(She takes it off.)

Rumplestiltskin:

I'll take it.

(He takes the bracelet.)

Now go to sleep.

When you wake up,

the straw will be gold.

Girl: All right.

(She sits down and closes her eyes.

Rumplestiltskin takes the straw

and tip-toes out.

Then he comes back with the gold.

He puts it on the table.

Then he tip-toes out again.)

Girl:

(She sits up and rubs her eyes.)

Oh! He really did it!

I'll show the king!

(She gets up and picks up the gold.

Then she goes out.)

Narrator:

The king was pleased.

But he was very greedy.

He wanted more gold.

So he gave the girl more straw.

And sent her back to the spinning room.

Girl: (She comes in

and puts the straw on the table.)

Oh dear!

I can't spin straw into gold.

What am I going to do now?

(She starts to cry.)

Rumplestiltskin: (He comes in.)

If you give me another present,

I will turn the straw into gold.

Girl:

But I don't have anything to give you!

Rumplestiltskin: Hmmm.

(He walks back and forth.)

I know.

When you become queen

you must give me your first baby.

Girl: (She laughs.)

Since I will never be queen

I can promise that.

Now turn the straw into gold.

(The girl sits down

and closes her eyes.

Rumplestiltskin takes the straw

and goes out.

He comes back with the gold

and puts it on the table.

Then he goes out again.)

Narrator:

When the girl woke up,

she took the gold to the king.

(The girl gets up.

She takes the gold and goes out.)

The king was so pleased

that he married the girl.

And she became the queen.

After a while, the queen had a baby.

(The queen comes in.

She is carrying the doll.)

Rumplestiltskin: (He comes in.)

Hello queen.

I've come to get

the baby you promised me.

(He holds out his hands.)

Queen:

Oh no! You can't take my baby!

Rumplestiltskin:

Oh yes I can. You promised!

Queen:

Won't you take something else

instead?

Rumplestiltskin:

No. But I will do this:

I will give you three days

to find out my name.

If you find out,

I will let you keep your baby.

(He goes out.)

Queen:

Oh dear!

How can I find out his name?

Oh dear!

Narrator:

The queen thought of all the names
she could.

At the end of the first day,

Rumplestiltskin came back.

(Rumplestiltskin comes in.)

Queen:

Is your name Jasper? Or Casper?

Or Albert?

Rumplestiltskin:

No! No! And no!

You have two more days!

(He goes out.

The queen sits quietly.)

Narrator:

The queen asked everyone

for all the names they knew.

At the end of the second day,

Rumplestiltskin came back.

(Rumplestiltskin comes in.)

Queen:

Is your name Spiderlegs?

Or Cowribs? Or Spindleshanks?

Rumplestiltskin:

No! No! And no!

You have one more day!

(He goes out.)

Narrator:

The queen sent her messengers

all over the land

to look for names.

(She goes out.)

At the edge of the woods

a messenger heard someone singing.

Rumplestiltskin: (He hops in singing.)

Ha! Ha! And ho! Ho!

My name the queen doesn't know.

Her baby I'm going to win,

sure as my name is Rumplestiltskin!

(He hops out.)

Narrator:

The messenger went to the queen

and told her what he had heard.

And at the end of the third day,

Rumplestiltskin came to see the queen.

(The queen comes in.

So does Rumplestiltskin.)

Queen:

Is your name Tom? Or Dick? Or Harry?

Rumplestiltskin:

No! It's not any of those!

Queen:

Well then,

is it RUMPLESTILTSKIN?

Rumplestiltskin:

(He hops up and down.

He spins around and yells.)

The devil must have told you!

The devil must have told you!

(He runs out.)

Narrator:

Rumplestiltskin never came back.

And the king and the queen

and their baby

lived happily ever after.

The end.

(He bows.)

GOBLIN'S MAGIC TRICK

Goblin bowed to Witch and Ghost.

"And now," Goblin said,

"I, Goblin the Great,

will do an amazing feat of magic.

It was taught to me

by a very famous magician.

44

He is known as Mr. Mysterious.

He has turned mountains

into humbugs

and humbugs into mountains."

"Think of that!" said Ghost.

"Oh my!" said Witch.

Goblin bowed again.

He picked up a pile of envelopes

from the table in front of him.

"You see these envelopes?" he said.

"Plain, ordinary envelopes."

"That's true," said Witch.

"I have some just like them."

"Shhh!" said Ghost.

There was a piece of newspaper

on the table.

It was the same size

as a dollar bill.

Goblin picked it up.

"You see this piece of paper?" he said.

"I, Goblin the Great, will show you
what magic can do to it. Watch!"

Goblin held the pile of envelopes.

Then he put the piece of paper

inside the top envelope.

"Now," Goblin said,

"Ghost, come up here.

Write your name

on the flap of the envelope."

Ghost wrote his name on the flap.

Then he sat down again.

Goblin showed Witch

the pile of envelopes.

She could see Ghost's name
on the flap.

"Now I'll seal the envelope,"
Goblin said.

"Then my magic will begin to work."
He pulled the flap
that had Ghost's name on it.
And that envelope came away
from the rest of the pile.

Goblin licked the flap

and sealed the envelope.

Then he handed it to Witch.

"Hold it tight, Witch," Goblin said.

"Then I'll say the magic words."

Witch held the envelope

as tight as she could.

Goblin said,

"ALA-KA-ZEE! ALA-KA-ZOO!

KA-RIN AND KA-RAN

PAPER INTO MONEY

AS FAST AS YOU CAN!"

And he snapped his fingers twice.

Then Goblin said,

"I, Goblin the Great,

have finished making my magic.

The paper is now MONEY.

Witch, you may open the envelope."

Witch opened it.

"Oh my!" she shouted.

"He really did it!"

Witch took a dollar bill

out of the envelope

and showed it to Ghost.

"Hooray for Goblin the Great!"

Ghost said.

And he clapped.

So did Witch.

Goblin bowed.

"How did you do it, Goblin?"
asked Ghost.

"Magicians shouldn't tell
their secrets," Goblin said.

"We won't tell anyone," Witch said.

"No," said Ghost, "not anyone."

Goblin looked at Witch and Ghost.

"Hmmm," he said. "All right."

And this is the secret Goblin told:

To do this magic trick

you have to "fix"

the pile of envelopes.

The top envelope has no flap.

It has been cut off.

The second envelope

has a dollar bill already in it.

The envelope without a flap

is placed on top

of the one with the dollar in it.

It is tucked under the flap

of the second envelope—

so that it looks like it has a flap.

The piece of newspaper

is put in the top envelope.

The flap that is pulled up

is really the flap

of the second envelope.

But it looks like

the flap of the top one.

So the envelope

that is pulled away from the pile

and sealed

is the one with the dollar bill

already in it!

WITCH'S SECRET CODE

"Look what I found, Witch,"

said Goblin.

"I have turned it every which way,

but I can't tell what it says."

And he showed Witch a piece of paper.

Witch looked at it.

Then she laughed.

"I know what it says," said Witch.

"I wrote it.

It's a message in secret code."

"Secret code!" said Goblin.

"Yes," said Witch.

"Only someone who knows the code
can read it."

"Oh," said Goblin.

"Would you like to learn
the secret code, Goblin?"
asked Witch.
"Oh yes!" Goblin said.
"All right," said Witch.
"I'll show you how it works."
Witch got a piece of paper
and a pencil.

"First," Witch said,

"you draw lines like this:

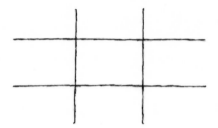

Then you put dots in. Like this:

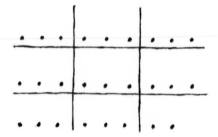

Each of the dots

stands for a letter of the alphabet.

a	b	c	d	e	f	g	h	i
•	•	•	•	•	•	•	•	•
j	k	l	m	n	o	p	q	r
•	•	•	•	•	•	•	•	•
s	t	u	v	w	x	y	z	
•	•	•	•	•	•	•	•	

When you write in code

you use both the lines and the dots.

The lines tell you

where to look for the letter.

The number of dots tell you

which letter it is.

Like this:

$$\square = n$$

To write a word you use

only the lines and dots

that you need.

Like this:

$$.] = S \quad \underline{..}] = k \quad [. = y$$

To write a sentence,

you put a slanted line

between each word.

Like this:

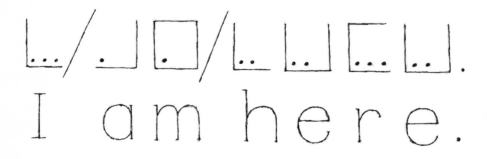

"I see how it works!" said Goblin.

"Now I'll write *you* a message

in the secret code!"

This is what Goblin wrote:

I am glad you are my friend.

Sue Alexander is a well-known writer of books and stories for children. She is on the board of directors of the Society of Children's Book Writers and the recipient of the 1980 Dorothy C. McKenzie Award given by the Southern California Council on Literature for Children. She has three grown children and lives with her husband in Canoga Park, California.

Jeanette Winter's portrayals of Witch, Goblin, and Ghost feature the same delicate deadpan impishness and droll humor that made her first picture book, *The Christmas Visitors*, an AIGA Children's Book of the Year. She lives with her husband and their two sons in Dallas, Texas.